Graceful Lives

Graceful Lives

Family Origins, Life Story, and Descendents of William and Grace Lassey

BILL LASSEY, MARILYN SACKMAN, AND MAVIS BERRY

iUniverse, Inc.
Bloomington

Graceful Lives
Family Origins, Life Story, and Descendents of William and Grace Lassey

iUniverse books may be ordered through booksellers or by contacting:

iUniverse
1663 Liberty Drive
Bloomington, IN 47403
www.iuniverse.com
1-800-Authors (1-800-288-4677)

Because of the dynamic nature of the Internet, any web addresses or links contained in this book may have changed since publication and may no longer be valid. The views expressed in this work are solely those of the author and do not necessarily reflect the views of the publisher, and the publisher hereby disclaims any responsibility for them.

Any people depicted in stock imagery provided by Thinkstock are models, and such images are being used for illustrative purposes only.
Certain stock imagery © Thinkstock.

ISBN: 978-1-4620-6796-1 (sc)
ISBN: 978-1-4620-6797-8 (ebk)

Printed in the United States of America

iUniverse rev. date: 11/18/2011

CONTENTS

INTRODUCTION

We are very proud of our grandparents, parents and extended family. They should all definitely have a place in history! This volume is our attempt to record all of the available information, and a collection of photographs, about the family. Information is largely drawn from family records including an extensive collection of albums prepared by our mother, Grace, over the years. We also had full access to records collected by siblings of both our parents. The editors also had personal collections of information that have contributed to this summary.

Information on Lassey and Clark name origins and history comes in part from the Ancestry.com, My Heritage.com, and the Personal Ancestry File (Mormon) websites, with data drawn from census records and other reputable sources.

The information on contemporary family was provided directly by family members, who also supplied some of the photographs. We are quite aware that by the time this is published some of the information will already be out-of-date, as the family continues to expand, jobs change, and events transpire to alter the status of many of us. This volume is thus a "benchmark" rather than a final statement of family history.

CHAPTER I

ORIGINS OF THE LASSEY FAMILY

In the year 2000, census records indicate that there were 61 Lassey family households in the United States, with the largest numbers residing in Washington (8), Florida (7), California (6), Kansas (6), and Massachusetts (6). There were at least four Lassey households in North Dakota at that time—down from at least six in 1950, all of whom were descendents of Constant and Emalie Lassey.

CONSTANT AND EMALIE LASSEY

Most people with the name Lassey who immigrated to the United States between 1840 and 1947 came from the United Kingdom. Constant and Emilie Lassey were an exception, when they moved permanently from Belgium in 1900. In fact, the 1920 Census listed only two Lasseys born in Belgium—which would have had to be Constant and Emilie. A few other Lasseys came from other locations in continental Europe. The record thus suggests that Lassey is largely a British name, probably adopted by Constant because it seemed more "American" than a Belgian name, which was "Lassui," (although this may not have been the exact spelling in Belgian). Adopting a simple and easily pronounced name was commonplace for immigrants to this country.

Constant (Stany) Lassey (or Lassui) was born in Caneghen, Belgium, May 24, 1868, to Ferdinand and Julie Verleye Lassoo (he had one sister, Marie, and one brother, Felix), and immigrated to the U.S. in the late 1890s, where he worked part of the time as a bricklayer and part of the time as a logger in Illinois. His original intention was to improve his education, which he was able to achieve, to 4th or 5th grade.

He returned briefly to Belgium in 1900, "to find a good Belgian wife" (as he and Emalie used to joke!). He met and, after a very short courtship (three days!), married Emalie Pieters on May 18, 1900 at Eighem, Belgium (arranged in part by her older sister, living in Michigan, who had requested that Emalie's family help Constant pick up a pair of earrings for her). Emalie was born on May 18, 1876, at Petham, Belgium, to Constant and Ludevica Verchatse Pieters. She had five brothers and four sisters (several of whom also immigrated, including Julius and Emma who lived in Cartwright). Her sister, Emeransa, married Camiel Deblaere; their grandson, Hedwig, visited Cartwright twice, and welcomed several members of the family to his home in Belgium. We kept in touch with him by e-mail until his recent death.

During the late 1800's, Belgium was a largely Catholic country, with the church having huge, and sometimes oppressive, influence on the government. There was little opportunity for education. Many people wanted to leave Belgium because there was so little opportunity to get ahead. One of the biggest industries was manufacturing linen lace. Emalie worked in the lace mills from the age of 6, until she was 26 years old and married Constant. For many years after Emalie came to the United States she would take out a "pillow" on which she made lace. Using many spools of linen thread she would toss them in such a way as to create a beautiful pattern of lace.

After arriving in the United States they initially settled at Seneca, Illinois, where their sons Julius, Raymond, and Frank were born. Having heard of the opportunity to secure free land, Constant traveled by rail to the Cartwright area in 1905 to stake a claim for a homestead north of town—even though he had contracted to buy 400 acres in Iowa (later sold). He returned to Illinois in 1906 to pick up his farm machinery and household goods which he transported to Cartwright by rail, accompanied by his brother, Felix, Martin Sandy, and Henry Tac. He began construction of a house, and adjoining barn, for his family. Emalie came by train in the spring with the three boys, reportedly bringing with her a cow, chickens, a corn seeder, and $1000 in cash (hidden in her sock, or bra!). Sophie was born May 8, 1906, three weeks after Emalie's arrival at Cartwright. Two other daughters arrived shortly thereafter, Martha on December 18, 1907, and Mary on November 8, 1909. Emil arrived June 1, 1911, William on March 2, 1914, and Morris on November 25, 1916.

Constant soon began to expand his initial 160 acre homestead, working the larger acreage with three teams, and a total of 24 work horses. He acquired his first tractor, a 30-60 Hart Parr, in 1909. While attempting to cross the Yellowstone River with it on the ice near Buford, it was almost lost because of rising water; he and his neighbors managed to get it to higher ground on a mat of willows. Using an Emerson plow, the tractor enabled him to break his own sod (soil that had not been previously farmed), and that of several neighbors. They bought their first car in 1914, for $200.

He also expanded his enterprise in 1916, purchasing the Sanitary Meat Market in Charbonneau, a few miles east of Cartwright. It included a house that was later moved to Cartwright (and became their retirement home in 1931). Julius and Frank helped with farming, and Raymond focused especially on the Charbonneau business, delivering meat, fish, and cheeses with a one-horse wagon in the Cartwright and Charbonneau area, until 1921 when they closed the business.

The farmstead was expanded with a round barn in 1918 (never entirely completed), a log barn, and improvements on the house, including a kitchen built of natural stone. Felix, Constant, and other neighbors, did a lot of mutual helping during building construction and other work on neighboring farms during busy seasons—a tradition that continued with other Lassey families in later years. He received the homestead of his brother, Felix (who died in 1920), and purchased two homesteads of other neighbors, also in 1920. He purchased a threshing machine with another neighbor, and was able to thresh crops for a group of neighbors in the nearby community.

Emalie and a friend returned to Belgium for a visit with relatives in 1924. While she was away, her children contracted mumps, measles, and small-pox, and were quarantined at home for six weeks!

Constant, and sons Julius and Frank, started the Lassey Implement Company in 1926, selling Hart Parr tractors, Nichols and Sheppard Combines, and later, the New Way Harvester (which cut the grain into small stacks for threshing) in Cartwright, Alexander, Fairview, and vicinity. Unfortunately, the implement business was not able to survive the Great Depression and drought of the early 1930's, when many farmers had to give up their farms and were not able to make payments on the equipment they had purchased.

After retiring at their home in Cartwright in 1931, Constant and Emalie turned the north farm over to Julius and Raymond, and the farm south of Cartwright (purchased in 1929 from the Bank of Minneapolis, after it was foreclosed) over to William and Grace. Frank purchased his own farm near Cartwright. Morris later purchased the north farm, and eventually sold it to a neighbor, Dennis Skorpil, when he retired from farming.

Constant and Emalie always planted large gardens, supplying vegetables to their family. Constant also helped out on the farms on a regular basis, assisting his grandson, Bill (in 1943), for example, to run a Hart Parr tractor while plowing. One of his primary activities was fishing in the

Yellowstone River, supplying the household with catfish and pike, much to the enjoyment of his son, daughter-in-law, and grandchildren!

Constant lived 85 years, until 1954, and Emalie lived 91 years, until 1967. Most of their family stayed in the immediate area, and continued the farming tradition. Julius married Victoria Potter (and later Ann Westfall), and also established an implement business in Williston; Julius and Victoria had two children, Charles and Bonnie. Raymond married Olga Johnson, and farmed until his premature death in 1934; they had two children, Merton (killed in a hunting accident in his 20s) and Ardell. Frank married Helen Dore, and farmed until his death; they had one son, Jerry.

Sophie married Art Overson (and later, Bert Youngstrom), and had two sons, Don and Clarence. Martha married Henry Winters (and later, Alex Carlson and John Bacon), and had two sons, Glenn and Stanley. Mary married Guy Shaide, who farmed near Cartwright; they had one son, Ronald. Emil married Marion Gangsted, and farmed north of Cartwright; they had three children, David, Allen, and Beverly. Morris married Lillian Thomas (and later, Ruthanne Beiri), and farmed the original expanded homestead north of Cartwright; he had three children, Sharon, Roger, and Charlotte.

The Constant Lassey Family. Top row left to right: Frank; Constant, Mary, Emalie and William. Morris, Sophie, Martha, Raymond, Julius. Front row: Emil.

CHAPTER 2

ORIGINS OF THE CLARK FAMILY

By some accounts, the Clark family history in the United States began with the arrival of Francis Eaton on the Mayflower sailing ship in 1620. Mr. Eaton was a signer of the Mayflower Compact, helping to establish one of the first organized non-native American communities at Plymouth, Massachusetts. He was said to be an early relative of General George Rogers Clark, the highest ranking American military officer on the northwestern frontier during the Revolutionary War. He was considered by some historians to be the "Conqueror of the Old Northwest." and certainly one of many notable Clarks in early American History. His younger brother, William Clark, was a leader of the famous Lewis and Clark Expedition that first explored the Northwest.

GEORGE W. CLARK

Grace Princess Clark Lassey's grandfather, George W. Clark, was also said to be a descendent of Francis Eaton, a relative of George Rogers Clark and William Clark, and was a notable Montana pioneer. He was born in Boston in 1846, and lived much of his life in the eastern part of the country. His wife, Elizabeth A. Pendell, was born in 1851, in Catskill, NY (they later divorced). Their son, Louie P. Clark, Grace's father, was born in Boston, Massachusetts, August 6, 1874. He migrated west and married Princess Hall in 1909 in Williston, ND. Princess was born in Osceola, Iowa in 1877. Her father, Samuel K. Hall, was born in 1837 in Guernsey, OH (and died in 1913, in Alexander, ND). Her mother, Princess O. Brown, was born in 1847 in Waterton, OH (and also died in Alexander, in 1915).

George W. Clark earned a reputation as an Indian fighter and a major contributor to the settlement of Montana after the Civil War. At age 15 he enlisted in the Union army, becoming a bugle boy. He got sick, and his young age was discovered, so he was discharged. He reenlisted at age 18, fought in the battle of Antieam, Virginia, in 1862, and later in several Florida battles, before his discharge in 1865. Ten years later in 1876 he reenlisted in the regular army and was sent west to Ogden, Utah, and then to Fort Ellis, Montana—arriving soon after the Battle of the Little Bighorn in 1876. He fought in the Battle of the Big Muddy in 1877 against the Minnehange Indians. He was sent to Fort Assiniboine where he served as head carpenter in construction at the Fort, completing the work in 1881. After discharge he returned to the East, working as a carpenter. In 1913 he returned to Montana to be near his two children, Jennie and Louie, and homesteaded at Three Buttes in Richland County. He died in 1937 at the age of 81 at Sidney, Montana.

LOUIE AND PRINCESS CLARK

Louie and Princess first discovered each other while working on a ranch near Sidney, Montana, in 1903. She was a tutor for the rancher's daughter, while he herded sheep and did other ranch tasks. She had been raised as a "southern lady" and dressed the part. He was immediately smitten with her and decided to continue working on the ranch for the remainder of the winter so he could be nearby. He established his Rawson, North Dakota, homestead in the spring of 1903; she followed him later, and also filed for a homestead.

They were married in 1909. During the first year they lived in the sod house belonging to Princess, but then added a frame house with two floors, using the sod room as a kitchen. Grace Princess was born on June 28, 1910, in Williston, ND. She was followed successively by Ruth (born in 1911), Beulah (1912), Kenneth (1914), Wayne (1916), and Dale (1917).

As was the case in most farm families, everyone contributed to the farm work when they were old enough, which included helping raise grain, milking 10 to 15 cows, and caring for pigs and chickens. The milk was separated from the cream, and fed to the calves. As she grew older, Grace also helped with the field work, proudly driving two horses on a dump rake, or mower, and on a wagon to haul grain to the elevator. Later, as her younger brothers grew old enough they took over the farming tasks.

All the children attended Valley View School in Rawson, and later, high school in Alexander, five miles away. Grace was a very good student from the outset, and was able to skip two grades in elementary school. She recalled many good teachers, but was particularly keen on one male teacher, G.G. Lane who was an outstanding teacher, despite the fact that he occasionally nipped from a liquor bottle during school hours. He thought so much of Grace that he wrote letters to her for a number of years after she graduated.

Louis and Princess moved from Rawson to the Burns Creek community west of Savage, Montana, in 1930, where they farmed until retiring to Sidney, Montana, in 1946—leaving the farm to their sons, Kenneth and Dale. Wayne worked in Sidney at the Holly Sugar Factory. Louis died in 1947, and Princess in 1956. Ruth married Everett Goldsmith, and had four children: Jean, Betty Lou, Richard, and John. Beulah first married Charley Smith, and later, Louie Yunek, and had two children: Princess (who died in childhood), and Melody. Kenneth married Eleanor Price, and had four children: LeRoy, Roger, Keith, and Kathy. Wayne did not get married. Dale married Verna Gebhardt, and had four children: Larry, Patsy, Carolyn, and Phyliss.

Grace Lassey's family: back L to R, Wayne Clark, Beulah Yunek, Grace Lassey, Ruth Goldsmith Kenneth Clark, front: Princess Clark, Dale Clark and Louie Clark

GRACE PRINCESS CLARK LASSEY

Grace and her sisters stayed in Alexander for high school during the week and went home on weekends, sometimes riding the "galloping goose," a one-car train. She worked for her room and board, at age 13, getting some strict guidance from her host family, Jack Smiths. She got very good marks, skipped two grade levels, and graduated at age 15, as Salutatorian, in 1925.

Her ambition was to be a teacher, and in grade eight she wrote an application to teach in a nearby school. After high school she went to Normal School (Teachers College) in Dickinson. Her parents gave her $100 to get started. She worked in the summer, cooking for a threshing crew among other tasks, and worked at several jobs while attending college.

After one year, she applied for a teaching position at Rogers School, four miles from Rawson. At age 17, she had 25 pupils in all eight grades her first year. She drove her parent's Model T Ford to school in good weather, and was transported by her father with horse and sleigh in winter. Part of the time during the week she lived two miles from the school with a family, and walked to her classes. She had to build and stoke the fire in a pot-bellied stove.

She went to college during the summer, earning her teaching certificate in two years. She then applied for a teaching job in Cartwright, with 32 students in all eight grades, earning $100 per month, plus $15 for maintaining the school building. She soon had assistance from a certain William Lassey, who lived nearby with his parents. He helped build the fire in the stove, and helped maintain the school, beginning a romance that lasted for 66 years until Grace's death in 1997. She and William were married December 27, 1932, at Sidney, in a double-wedding ceremony with her sister, Ruth, and Everett Goldsmith.

William and Grace Lassey's wedding picture

William and Grace: 50-years later

CHAPTER 3

THE LIFE STORY OF
WILLIAM AND GRACE LASSEY

After their marriage, William and Grace moved to the farm south of Cartwright, where they lived throughout their lives. William and his father had earlier built a two-room cottonwood log house near the river. After the addition of a frame kitchen, they resided in the same house for the first thirteen years. There was an outhouse for the natural requirements, and no running water or electricity for the entire time they lived there. They depended instead on a windmill by the river, with water hauled uphill by hand, and kerosene or gas lamps for light.

All three of their older children were born in the one bedroom of the log house, with the assistance of Grace's mother, Princess, and later, Dr. Harrold from Fairview, a chiropractic physician, who arrived after Lila had already been born (delivered by Grandpa Constant Lassey!) in 1933. Bill came on the scene in 1934 and Marilyn was born in 1936. Mavis was a little tardy, arriving 13 years after Marilyn, in 1949, at the Sidney hospital.

The old log house that Grandpa Lassey and William built.

Grace's sense of community responsibility was already evident. She was very active in a variety of local leadership activities, in her church, with the Parent Teachers Association, playing the piano for dances at the local hall, and in many other service roles. She taught at Cartwright three years, until Lila was born. Later, after Marilyn's birth, she began teaching at Horse

Creek School south of Cartwright, for $50 per month. Her sister Beulah helped care for Lila, Bill, and Marilyn.

Because of the severe drought of the mid-1930s, and the national economic depression that led to minimal tax funds to support schools, teacher's salaries had been cut drastically; Grace sometimes received only a warrant that could be cashed later when the school district had money. Nonetheless, she continued to teach throughout the period when her children were in school, until her first retirement. After ten years at home on the farm, she returned to teaching while in her 50's, in part to take advantage of a new teacher's retirement law that she helped to implement while on the State Teachers Retirement Board. By serving a few more years she was able to qualify for teacher's retirement and social security income, neither of which was available during her earlier years in the profession.

The contrast between her early teaching years, and her final years, was quite profound. As noted above, at her first school she had to travel by wagon or sled, and sometimes walk part way, then had to carry in wood and coal, and build fires, in a pot-bellied stove. She had to scrub and oil a rough wooden floor, and accomplish all the other janitorial work. She had 20 to 30 students in one room. In the later years at East Fairview, she had about 20 students, all in the same grade, ate hot lunches from the school cafeteria, enjoyed the assistance of full-time janitors, and often taught children whose parents she had taught in her earlier years.

She had a wonderful reputation as a teacher. As Lila wrote in a tribute written for her 80th birthday, "she always had a marvelous way with children. She seemed to have an uncanny knack for discipline. I was always amazed at how she handled grandchildren. She was always firm, never letting them get away with anything; yet they adored her . . . The children respected and loved her. She had a way of bringing out the very best in children." As Mavis said in a high school English class essay in 1964 about mothers, "I wish everyone else could have a mother as wonderful as mine!"

In the early years, it was difficult to make a living on the farm. In 1934, when Bill was born, there was no crop at all. William rowed across the river in an old boat during the summer where he thinned and topped beets for $1 per day. He also cooked for a fence post cutting crew that was building fences for the nearby government pasture. On the farm, they raised 150 pigs that were of so little value that they traded some of them for beet tops to feed the cattle when very little grass was available. He also traded pigs for vegetables to feed the family. Some had to be given away because there was no market for them. Full-grown sows were worth only $3.

Farming was largely accomplished with horses, at this stage. A neighboring rancher loaned William young horses, which he broke and trained for the privilege of using them, later returning them to the owner. A Hart Parr tractor belonging to the Lassey family was used for plowing and threshing—as a cooperative venture with family and neighbors.

William eventually got a job with the Government Land Utilization Program (part of President Roosevelt's New Deal) in 1935, working for $45 per month to help develop water supplies for the government pastures all around McKenzie County. He quickly became foreman (at $55 per month) of a crew of men from the area who also needed employment during those dry years.

Grace and Willie Lassey, Marilyn, Lila and Bill by the old windmill

William and Grace prospered sufficiently that they were able to purchase their farm (283 acres) in 1942 from Constant for $1500. They later purchased additional adjoining land in 1948 and 1950, including what was known as "The Scrivner Place," bringing the total to 872 acres. They continued to raise grain, pigs, and cattle, purchasing some of their first Hereford cattle for $11 per head from a neighbor. They purchased dairy cows that produced milk for home use, as well as butter for sale to the Cartwright Mercantile. They acquired their own Model B John Deere tractor in 1942. William continued to do various other activities to earn extra income, such as selling Farmers Union Insurance to his neighbors, and appraising land.

William Lassey's old "B" John Deere Tractor and corn planter

They moved a house, purchased from his brother, Julius, and built extra rooms, in 1945, replacing the log cabin (later converted to a chicken coop). Indoor plumbing was introduced soon after, and they produced their own electricity with a generator—until the advent of the Rural Electrification Administration a few years later. In 1982, they built a spacious new house immediately east of their second house.

William and Grace Lassey's home on the farm

One incident that has become part of the family folklore occurred when Grace took Lila with her to the school picnic, ten miles from home. Bill and Marilyn, age 4 and 3, having been left at home with a hired girl, decided to walk down the road to meet their mother—which they eventually did about five miles from home! Grace was shocked to see them along the road, and picked them up for the return home. Meanwhile, the hired girl had gone to the road and stopped cars, asking for help in finding the missing kids. Neighbors were everywhere searching along the river, in haystacks, and wherever they thought the missing kids might be found. Needless to say, everyone, especially Grace and the hired girl, was happy to know they had been found!

Lives of Service and Leadership

William and Grace were continuously active in the community, statewide, and even nationally. William served on the Farmers Union Oil Company Board of Directors for 28 years, including several years as President.

He was Inspector in charge of elections for 35 years, was Director and Executive Director of the McKenzie County Grazing Association for 30 years, and was appointed by North Dakota Governor Arthur Link, to the Regional Advisory Board for the Trails West Committee. Later, he served on the State Advisory Board of the North Dakota Rangeland Resource Program. He served many years as vestryman and warden for the Episcopal Church in Cartwright, was on the Governing Board and President of Sioux Farmers Union local, and as a trusted local citizen, was appointed to administer the estates of several neighbors after their deaths. In other instances, as noted earlier, he was employed as an appraiser for evaluating the value of land. He helped organize the Cartwright Irrigation District with neighboring farmers. The district pumped from wells and distributed water through a network of ditches. He was the first District secretary (with his wife's help!).

Grace served for many years as county Secretary of the Farmers Union and was also Educational Leader. Among her duties was organization of youth camps in the summer at North Roosevelt National Park and other locations (her children attended several of the camps). She served six years on the State Teachers Insurance and Retirement Board of Trustees, the last three as Chairperson. She was Treasurer of the Estes School District for ten years and was Secretary-Treasurer of the Episcopal Church for nearly 20 years, as well as the primary organist. She was a member and officer of the Sunshine Homemakers Club for 40 years.

She was the local census-taker, an election board member for 40 years, and was always active in the Democratic Party, as regional director for Western North Dakota, and supporter of many candidates for office. Several governors publicly recognized her many contributions with letters of commendation.

Although she did not receive a B.S. degree, she took courses during summers to increase her qualifications, always trying to improve her knowledge and skills. She taught a total of 28 years. Her final seven years included three years at Keene, and four years at East Fairview School, where she retired when she was 60 years of age. Hundreds of students, including her four children, benefited from her outstanding teaching skill and strong commitment to high quality education.

William was the first farmer in the area to invest in a "tractor move" sprinkler irrigation system (the pipes could be moved by hooking onto them with a tractor), pumping water from the Yellowstone River, and later from wells, while substantially increasing the productivity of the farm. They were able to enlarge their cattle herd, using a permit to pasture livestock in the adjacent government cattle reserve. His innovation with sprinkler irrigation was a subject of much discussion in the community, and became the topic of young Bill's speech that won second place in the Future Farmers of America state-wide competition in Bozeman. Soon, other farmers were adopting the same practice.

Among their other achievements was an award as Conservation Achievement winner from the Lower Yellowstone Soil Conservation District in 1976. They were honored at the state Soil Conservation Convention in Fargo, received an award certificate, and were presented with a color photo of their farm taken from an airplane. Several magazine and newspaper articles were written about their farming and ranching achievements.

Because of their leadership at the local, county, and state levels, they were selected as delegates to several national Farmers Union Conventions around the country, and were local representatives to several state political conventions. As their prosperity increased, they traveled extensively in the continental United States, as well as Alaska, Hawaii, Canada, Mexico, the Caribbean Islands, and Europe. Bill was on sabbatical leave in the Netherlands and was able to escort them to several European countries, including a visit with some of William's Belgian relatives.

They were always a team, working together to solve innumerable challenges, while creating in the process a happy and productive household. They were the central elements of an extended family, pillars of the Cartwright community, and major contributors to their county, state, and nation.

Grace and William Lassey and extended family

CHAPTER 4

CHILDREN, GRANDCHILDREN, AND
GREAT GRANDCHILDREN

LILA WINIFRED LASSEY STEWART

Lila was born July 10, 1933, in the log house by the Yellowstone River, and started first grade at Estes School, with her mother as teacher. She started high school in Sidney, but transferred to Fairview as a sophomore, graduating in 1951. Her first job was with an abstracting company in Watford City, working on oil leases. She and Jim Stewart were married in 1952 while he was working at the Safeway Super Market in Sidney. The company moved him to several other locations in Montana, as a manager, including Livingston, Miles City, Kalispell, and Greybull, Wyoming. Lila also worked for an abstracting firm in Sidney, and for a plumbing company in Miles City when they moved there. They had five children: Linda, Charlene, Karen, Cindy, and Tim.

Later in life, she worked as a server in several restaurants, largely in Miles City and Williston, where she also worked at Penney's clothing store. After retirement from the restaurant business, she managed a senior living facility in Miles City until she was disabled by diabetes and other health problems. She moved to Bismarck in search of better medical care, and lived in a Baptist assisted living facility—until her health condition forced her to enter the nursing home unit at the same facility. She died there on January 11, 2010, at age 76.

Lila Stewart and her extended family

Linda Renee Stewart Wildman

Linda was born on May 17, 1953 in Sidney. She went to elementary school in Greybull, WY, and Miles City, graduating from high school in 1971 in Miles City. She went to Miles Community College but did not complete a degree. She married Dallas W. Wildman July 7, 1973.

She has been employed with the City of Miles City for 37 years, working in the Treasurer's office eight years, Engineering/Operations five years, and then as Deputy City Clerk. She was asked to assume the City Clerk position in 2007 but declined, and retired in June, 2008. However, she soon returned, as part-time Deputy City Clerk. She intended to work for a couple years and permanently retire. However, she has been involved in training two different City Clerks and an Assistant Deputy. Now she expects to work another year or so for the City, and then says she might try something else. Dallas is a hair stylist and operates his own salon.

Linda and Dallas have two children, Jodi Rene, born December 20, 1975, in Miles City, and Jenny Lynn, born July 1, 1980, also in Miles City. Both went to elementary school and high school in Miles City, Jodi graduating in 1994, and Jenny in 1998. Jodi went on to Miles Community College where she earned an Associate Degree in Medical Technology. Jenny went to Montana State University in Billings, earning an Elementary Education degree in 2002, and a Masters in Special Education in 2003.

Jodi married Theodore John Herzog on June 15, 1996. They have three children: Benjamin Chase, born September 1, 1995; Gavin Wade, born February 13, 1998; and Hope Renee, born March 15, 2002. Jodi has worked as a Medical Transcriptionist at the Veteran's Administration Medical Center, as an Assistant Financial Aid Officer at Miles Community College, and as a Program Technician at the USDA Farm Service Agency. Ted has worked for the USDA—Fort Keogh Agriculture and Research Station, at AgriBasics, at Blue Rock Distributing Company, and at the Montana Department of Transportation. Jodi says her family and kids are more important to her than the work she does. Her favorite forms of leisure activity are: church projects, bible study, reading, pilates, power cycling, scrapbooking, boating, walking, attending children's sporting and other events, and camping.

Jenny married Brad William Malloy on June 21, 2008. They have two daughters, Emma Rose, born on June 27, 2009, and Grace Hinsley, born in July, 2011. Jenny was a Special Education teacher in Bozeman from 2004 to 2008, and is now teaching in Livingston. Brad was a Physical Therapist in Dillon, MT, from 2001 to 2006, and is now practicing at the hospital in Livingston. They enjoy spending quality time with Emma and Grace, and also like to golf, hike, read, watch movies, try new activities, and just enjoy each other's company. They are church members and try to participate in the activities that are offered. They also enjoy spending time with their extended family in Miles City and North Dakota.

Linda's most valued accomplishments include, in her own words:

"I am proud of my relationships with my family; husband, children, grandchildren, parents, siblings, grandparents, aunts, uncles, cousins! That is more important to me than any career. These relationships bring me pride, happiness and a sense of peace far outweighing any career accomplishments. I can leave this world someday knowing I gave and had love in my life. To me, that is a life well lived!" Favorite forms of recreation: spending time with children/grandchildren; following grandchildren in sports; walking; time with friends; and flower gardening.

Charlene Kay Stewart Gunther

Charlene was born July 2, 1954, in Sidney. She went to elementary school in Greybull, WY, and Miles City, and graduated from high school in Miles City in 1972. She attended Miles Community College and earned an Associate of Arts Degree in 1981. She married Terry Lee Gunther on October 30, 1976. They have two children, Michelle LeAnn, born November 14, 1981 in Miles City, and Ryan Thomas, born June 1, 1986.

Michelle is married to Gary Hirsch, and works as a Dental Assistant in Miles City. Gary was born June 17, 1981, and works as a Combination Technician for Mid-Rivers Communication in Miles City. They have two children, Tristan Scott, born January 31, 2001, and KayLee Marie, born November 7, 2004. Ryan also works as a Combination Technician for Mid-Rivers in Miles City.

Charlene worked at the Safeway Supermarket in Miles City from 1972 to 1974, before joining the U.S. Army for a two-year tour (1974-76), part of the time in Germany. After discharge, she took a job with the Veterans Administration Medical Center in Miles City in 1976, working at a series of jobs, including Medical Administrator, Purchasing Agent,

Dental Secretary, Dental Assistant, as Supervisor for Patient Assistance, and as a Patient Advocate. In 2000 she transferred to the Bureau of Land Management as a Purchasing Agent/Contracting Officer in Billings. She held an ancillary position as an Equal Economic Opportunity Counselor at the Veteran's Administration and Bureau of Land Management for 18 years. Part of this job was training other Counselors in a four-state region. In 2010 she retired from Federal service after 36 years. Terry worked in the grocery business for 34 years, until 2006, when he took a job in Shipping and Receiving for Juco's Medical Supply in Billings.

Charlie's proudest accomplishment is her 36 years of federal service. She says her greatest achievement was raising two wonderful and successful children during her 35-years of marriage to Terry. She and Terry are avid "rummage sale" fans. Terry collects railroad memorabilia, which Charlie also enjoys. She loves reading and bible study, enjoys spending time with friends and family, and loves to bargain shop. She also volunteers at the Veterans Administration Clinic, and at her church.

Karen Grace Stewart Whitney

Karen was born May 10, 1957 in Sidney. She went to high school in Miles City, and married Tracey Lee Whitney, July 19, 1975, with whom she has four children.

Julie Ann was born May 17, 1974, and is married to Thomas Billig. They have four children: Christopher Michael Leatherman, born October 4, 1997; Carlee Irene Leatherman, born June 13, 1999; Codi Allen Leatherman, born April 11, 2002; and Brayden Thomas Billig, born October 4, 2006. Julie is a registered nurse.

Shawn Ryan was born November 29, 1978, and is married to Jamie Schmidt. They have three children: Dustin Ryan, born September 23,

1999; Brett Michael, born April 16, 2004; and Noah Isaak, born April 27, 2011. Shawn is self-employed and has a company called InLine Designs.

Nicholas James was born February 13, 1981, and has one son: Ayden Lee. He works as a Pumper/Roustabout for Steier Oil Services.

Melissa Marie was born July 23, 1983, and has a son, Alexander James Woyen, born May 14, 2005. She works for Aetna Life and Health as a Senior CSR.

Karen has worked from home for Aetna Life and Health since 1998. Earlier, she was Building and Operations Manager for the Jamestown Civic Center, was Office Manager for James River Senior Citizen Center, and did radio advertising sales. Tracy is currently Loan Officer/Manager for Dakota Certified Development Corporation (SBA Loans), and was previously self-employed doing consulting with the Regional Councils for Bismarck and Jamestown, and Lucas Aerospace.

Karen considers her four children and her 36-year marriage as her proudest accomplishments. She enjoys gardening, fishing, and other activities in the great outdoors.

Cindy Stewart Klym

Cindy was born in Greybull, WY on December 11, 1961, and went to elementary school in Kalispell, MT, and Jamestown, ND. She graduated from Williston High School in 1980. She received an Associate Degree in Elementary Education from the University of North Dakota-Williston in 1982, and earned her B.A. Degree in Business Administration from Minot State University in 1984.

She married Donald Christopher Klym on November 24, 1990. Don received his BBA Degree in Marketing from the University of North Dakota—Grand Forks, in 1984. They have four children: Christopher William, born on June 24, 1994, now a senior in high school; Whitney Princess, born August 10, 1996, now a high school freshman; Sarah Jean, born January 27, 1998, now an 8th grader; and Amanda Lee, born April 8, 2002, now a 3rd grader.

Don and Cindy are owners of The Painter Incorporated, with nine full-time employees—doing commercial and residential painting and wood finishing contracts in Bismarck and vicinity for the last 18 years. Cindy manages the office, including accounting, payroll, purchasing, and vehicle maintenance, while Don manages the contract bidding, supervises and schedules employees, and does the public relations required to enhance the business. Earlier in her career, Cindy was Office Coordinator for Public Affairs at the University of Mary for six years (1996-2002); served as Account Executive for Quality Printing Service in Bismarck (1993-1996); worked as Receptionist/Secretary at First National Bank in Gillette, WY (1992-1993); and was Personnel Director and Secretary to the Publisher of the Williston Daily Herald (1988-1992). Don was northeast Territorial Manger for the Casper Star Tribune (1992-1993); Circulation Manager and Mailroom Supervisor for the Williston Daily and Sunday Herald (1987-1992), and earlier, was a Real Estate Salesman in Cape Girardeau, MO (1985-1987).

Cindy is especially proud of her 20-year marriage to Don, while raising her four children in a Christian environment. Both Cindy and Don are very pleased with their successful business. Cindy likes gardening, walking, and reading. They both like boating and fishing, as well as going to the children's activities, and enjoying family life.

Tim J. Stewart

Tim was born June 14, 1966, in Miles City, Montana, where he also went to elementary school and high school. He received a degree in Business Administration, with a marketing major, from Minot State University in July, 1991. He has worked in a Bugle Boy Outlet, with several new and used auto and parts sales in Minot and Bismarck, as a Conductor Trainee for Burlington Northern Santa Fe Railway, as a service advisor in an auto dealership, and more recently in truck part sales.

He served in the North Dakota National Guard beginning in 1985, retiring in 1992 as a Sargent E-5. He participated in a variety of National Guard community service projects, and in the development of the Ft. Buford Historical Site. He enjoys motor cycle riding, golfing, traveling, and spending time with his family.

WILLIAM RAYMOND LASSEY

Bill was born September 27, 1934, in the log house by the Yellowstone River, as noted earlier. His elementary years were at Estes School, and then at Cartwright, with half of those years taught by his mother. He went to high school in Fairview, graduating in 1952 as Salutatorian, followed by four years of college at Montana State University, where he received his B.S. degree in Agricultural Economics in 1956. He was selected as an International Farm Youth Exchange student, spent six months visiting Turkey and other parts of Europe, and then toured Montana for six months using colored slides and commentary to report on his trip. He was drafted into the U.S. Army in 1957, spending most of his time at Fort Gordon, Augusta, Georgia. He married Mickey Hogarty while at home on leave.

After discharge, he joined a graduate program in international development at Montana State University in 1959, and received his Master's Degree in Agricultural Economics in 1961. He was then invited to study for his Ph.D. in Communication at Michigan State University; he spent two years in Costa Rica, with his family, working for the University and the Rockefeller Brothers Fund on a research program, while collecting data for his dissertation.

After completing Ph.D. studies, he was offered a job in the Department of Agricultural Economics and Rural Sociology at Montana State University in 1963, where he worked for the next ten years—the last year of which was on sabbatical leave in The Netherlands and United Kingdom. He took a position in the Department of Rural Sociology at Washington State University in 1973.

He and Marie Sellars were married December 3, 1973, in Vancouver, Washington. Marie has a B.S., M.S., and Ph.D. from the University of Utah, and taught two years at Weber State University in Ogden, UT. She was on the faculty in the Department of Sociology and Anthropology at the University of Idaho in Moscow for 22 years. During 26 years in the Northwest, Bill and Marie lived at various times in Pullman, Washington, Moscow, Idaho, and Spokane, Washington—where Bill was helping to develop a new university campus in downtown Spokane. They spent a year on sabbatical leave at Louisiana State University, and a year each in Asia and Europe teaching on U.S. military bases for the University of Maryland.

Marie retired in 1996, and Bill in 1999. They bought a new motor home, and spent much of their early retirement years traveling the country, with Tucson, AZ, as their home base. In 2010 they moved to Scottsdale, AZ, where they now live. (Further details are available in their memoirs, *Fabulous Journey*, published in 2008 by iUniverse).

Their proudest professional accomplishments include: authoring nine published books, writing dozens of published articles, and teaching thousands of successful students. As parents they take particular pride in their extended family and the continuing accomplishments of their five children. They enjoy traveling, reading, writing, dining at nice restaurants, walking, picnicking, and generally appreciating the beautiful desert environment in which they now live.

Norma Dione Lassey Greenberg

Dione was born November 14, 1958, in Augusta, Georgia. She attended elementary school and high school largely in Belgrade, Montana, taking one year away to travel with her parents in Europe where she attended Dutch and British schools. She graduated from high school in 1976, and attended Montana State University, receiving her degree in English Literature in 1980. She joined "Up With People" for a year of singing and entertaining in Europe, before starting graduate work. She received her M.A. degree in Art Therapy at Wright State University in Dayton, Ohio in 1988; her M.Ed. in Education at Antioch University McGregor in Yellow Springs, Ohio, in 2007; and a Certification in Gifted Education from the University of Cincinnati in 2008. She is an accomplished artist, with a large collection of paintings and other art work to her credit.

She married Dr. Saul Greenberg in 1993 in Yellow Springs, OH, where they continue to live. He has been a Professor on the faculty of Antioch University McGregor for the last seven years, and she has taught gifted middle school students at Xenia Community Schools, in Xenia, Ohio for the past five years. Earlier, Dione was Associate Director of the Center for Arts for the Disabled and Handicapped 5 years. Their daughter, Mollie Grace, was born on December 24, 1996, and now attends Miami Valley School in Dayton, where she completed the eighth grade in 2011. She is studying Mandarin Chinese, and spent three weeks in China with her teachers and school mates in June, 2011.

2/18/2011

Dione and Saul have planted much of their yard to garden, and raise much of their own food. They heat their home with a wood stove, and do their best to minimize impact on the environment. Dione writes a blog called FindingOurFamilyFootprint.blogspot.com. They are active in the Yellow Springs Community, and enjoy following Mollie's many activities at Miami Valley School.

Dione's proud accomplishments, in her own words:

"Mother—I am proud of the way we have raised Mollie. She is turning out to be an outstanding student academically, and she is also a great person! I stayed home to raise her and I'm proud of the fact that I took the time and energy to give her what she needed as a young child.

"Movin' On"—I choreographed and directed the Movin' On dance troupe for 7 years. This troupe was comprised of adults with developmental disabilities and we performed throughout the state of Ohio and at the Kennedy Center in Washington D.C. We worked with high caliber professional dancers including the Dayton Ballet and we performed for many local schools and organizations. We also met Henry Winkler, Kenny Rogers, and many other prominent actors and artists.

"Gifted Teacher"—I switched careers at age 48 and started teaching gifted middle school students. Every year I have been chosen as the favorite teacher of one of our "Hall of Fame" students who are honored by all the teachers. I give a speech every year to induct one of these students into the Hall of Fame. I have developed the gifted program into a solid activity that meets the needs of the students at our school.

"Professional Artist"—I have had solo exhibits of my artwork in a number of galleries in the area and have sold many pieces throughout the years.

"Gardner"—I love working in our garden, and we have had tours of our developing "Edible Forest Garden." I continue to take workshops and learn about the art of gardening and I really enjoy it! I also like walking and biking with Saul and Mollie."

Maureen Joy Lassey Rude

Maureen was born April 26, 1962, in East Lansing, Michigan. She attended elementary and high school largely in Belgrade, Montana, and for one year attended Dutch and British schools while her father was on sabbatical leave. She graduated from high school in 1980, and attended the University of Montana where she graduated in 1985 with a Bachelor of Science degree in Business Administration, with an emphasis in Accounting. She is a Certified Public Accountant. While completing her academic work, she worked for United Parcel Service for two years.

She took a job with the legislative auditing department for the State of Montana in 1985, where she worked for six years in Helena. She met her future husband, Matthew Charles Rude there, and they were married on July 22, 1989. She was appointed as Director of the Montana Board of Housing, serving for nine years, before accepting a position with Fannie Mae, the national home loan company, where she stayed eight years. She then took a job as Director of Operations with NeighborWorks Montana in 2009. Mat worked for the State of Montana in various administrative capacities over 30 years, retiring in 2009. He now works for the Rocky Mountain Development Council, focusing particularly on housing programs.

Maureen is proud to have received the Governor's Award for Excellence in Leadership, and was selected to be in the first class of Leadership Montana—a training program for up-and-coming state leaders. She also takes pride in having been part of building an organization that provides homebuyer education, counseling and down-payment assistance for homebuyers In all parts of Montana.

They live in the "country" twelve miles from Helena, where they enjoy hanging out with their dogs (Sosmo, Wiser, and Gordon), raising a greenhouse garden, reading, good music, and maintaining their beautiful home. Boating is among their favorite forms of recreation, especially hosting friends and family on trips through the "Gates of the Mountains" on the Missouri River. They love to travel, and closely follow University of

Montana Grizzly football games, as well as Boston Red Sox baseball, and enjoy great live music at concerts around the area and at home.

Marie's Children

Bill's family also includes **Sherry Hassard**, now a retired counselor and teacher living in Pullman, Washington; **Derek Sellars**, a quality control supervisor with the Iowa Department of Transportation, who lives in Oskaloosa, Iowa; and **Dara Sellars**, an administrator in Central Kitsap School District, who lives in Bremerton, Washington.

MARILYN GRACE LASSEY PROPP SACKMAN

Marilyn was born in the log house by the river on January 5, 1936, attended her first elementary school years at Estes School, with her mother as teacher, and completed elementary school in Cartwright. She graduated from Fairview High School in 1953. Later on she attended Williston State College.

She married Edward Propp on November 27, 1953. They had four children: Rodney, born August 25, 1954; Susan, born September 12, 1955; Carol, born January 5, 1957; and Julie, born October 19, 1965.

Marilyn and Eddie Propp and family, Rod, Susan Carol, and Julie

Eddie was an outstanding farmer throughout his life, often securing the highest beet yields in the valley. He served on many agricultural organization boards, and was a member and president of the Jaycees. He died of a brain tumor at the age of 39. Marilyn later married Isidor Sackman on June 24, 1998. He was a rancher and county commissioner until his retirement. He died in 2011.

Marilyn worked for the State of Montana, Division of Planning, for four years. She then worked as News Anchor, Sales Manager, and General Manager of KXMD Television in Williston for 20 years. She continues to manage her own rental apartments and houses in Sidney and Williston.

One of her proudest achievements was being named Salesperson of the Year in the State of Montana by the Montana Broadcaster's Association in 1984, which included a $10,000 award. Over the years she has enjoyed country western and ballroom dancing, and is always up for a great game of pinochle!

Rodney Propp

Rodney graduated from Sidney High School in 1972, and was named the only Merit Scholar at the time in Montana, with a scholarship to Montana State University in Bozeman. He then continued his college work at Washington State University and the University of Montana. He moved back to Fairview to engage in his first love, which was farming, until his death in 1988.

Marilyn's Family - L to R, Julie Goebel, Susan Welnel, Marilyn, Carol Sandvik and Rod Propp

Susan Marie Propp Welnel

Susan was born September 12, 1955, at Community Memorial Hospital in Sidney, and attended Central Elementary School. She went to high school for three years in Sidney, but attended her senior year at Fairview High School, where she graduated in 1973. She was very persistent about attending college over many years, including: Billings Business College (1973); University of North Dakota-Williston (1976); Dawson Community College (1993-94—night classes); University of North Dakota-Williston

(1995); University of Mary (1996-1997); the University of North Dakota (1998-2000), where she earned her B.A. in Clinical Psychology, Summa Cum Laude. She pursued graduate work at the Minnesota School of Professional Psychology at Argosy University (2001-2006), where she earned her M.A. and Doctorate in Clinical Psychology.

She married Harvey Albert Welnel on June 3, 1989, and has one daughter, Rebecca Sue Kvande, born March 11, 1980, and two grandchildren, Gabriel (age 8), and Mildred (age 1).

She has practiced as a Clinical Psychologist at Mayo Clinic Health System in Albert Lea, Minnesota since 2008. Earlier she practiced at MeritCare, Thief River Falls, MN (2007-2008), Minnesota Consortium for Advanced Rural Psychology Training (Post Doctorate—2006-2007), Central Iowa Veteran's Administration (Internship—2005-2006), Joslin Diabetes Center at Harvard University Medical School/University of Minnesota Neurobehavioral Technician (2004-2005), and worked for Christopherson Properties (2001), Statder Center Psychiatric Hospital (2000-2001), and Montana Dakota Utilities (1990-1995).

Harvey has worked at Christopherson Properties as Project Supervisor (2001-present); at Schuett Properties (1998-2000); at Sidney Country Club (1986-1998); and at Welnel Drilling (1972-1986).

Susan is very proud of having finally earned a doctorate after many years of effort. "The experience certainly changed my life, as well as the experiences of my family. During that journey, there were several highlights. I was part of a longitudinal study seeking to understand if the treatment of diabetes affected central nervous system functioning. I was hired to administer the neuropsychological test batteries on all the Minnesota participants. The results were later published in the New England Journal of Medicine. It was fun to be a small part of such important research.

Before I earned my doctorate, I was given the President's Leadership Award at Argosy University. This was something my professors voted on. I was involved in numerous graduate activities outside of classes, such as Student Senate and Student Member of the Institutional Review Board, but I had no idea that they viewed me as a leader! It was a proud moment for Harvey and me. I could not have accomplished much of this without the support of Harvey.

Finally, I am proud of my family. We have had many hurdles in life, and have never had to worry about being there for each other." Favorite forms of recreation: "I love flower and vegetable gardening, spending time outdoors, reading (my book collection is almost bordering on hoarding), horse racing, fishing, camping, traveling and spending time with friends and family."

Carol Propp Sandvik

Carol was born January 5, 1957 in Sidney, and graduated from Fairview High School in 1975. She has worked as a sales representative for KDSR Radio, and as Sales Manager at KXMD Television in Williston. She managed her own restaurant and bar at Oriska, North Dakota, and was later manager of a furniture store in Jamestown.

More recently she moved to Sidney, where she took care of her grandfather during his final days, and later has worked as a casino operator and administrator for an oil services business. She has a son, Brady Gene Berndt, born July 24. 1980, who currently works in sales in Minneapolis. Her daughter, Jennifer Rae Sandvik, was born November 14, 1990, and completed her Associate Degree at Bismarck State College in 2011—with plans to continue her education at Valley City State.

Julie Mae Propp Goebel

Julie was born in Sidney on October 19, 1965. She went to elementary school at East Fairview, and graduated from Williston High School in 1984. She attended the University of North Dakota at Grand Forks and Williston, The University of Wisconsin at Lacrosse, and completed her B.A. Degree in 2002, as well as an M.S. Degree in 2004, in Audiology from Minot State University. She earned a Doctor of Audiology from Salus University, Atkins Park, Pennsylvania in 2007, and is now a practicing Audiologist in Williston and Minot.

She is proud to have completed two half-marathons, and to have raised two wonderful children! Her favorite forms of recreation and relaxation are camping, running, gardening, and spending time with her family.

Her son, Daniel Edward Goebel, was born December 17, 1982. He earned a B.S. degree in Industrial Technology at the University of North Dakota in 2008, and is a Quality Control Engineer at Goodrich Corporation in Jamestown. Daughter Ashley Nicole Goebel was born April 24, 1991, and completed her cosmetology training in 2011. She intends to pursue a B.S. degree in Education.

Marilyn and her daughters, Susan Welnel, Marilyn, Julie Goebel and Carol Sandvik

Marilyn's Grandchildren, back, L to R, Dan Goebel, Becky Kvande, Brady Berndt
Front: Jennifer Sandvik and Ashley Goebel

MAVIS IRENE LASSEY BERRY

Mavis was born May 7, 1949, in the Sidney hospital. She attended elementary school at Pleasant Center (north of Cartwright), Horse Creek (south of Cartwright), and East Fairview, and graduated from Fairview High School in 1967. She attended business college in Billings.

She married Ronnie L. Berry November 11, 1967, while he was serving in the Marine Corps—after he had returned from a tour in Viet Nam. They lived for two years in California near his Marine base, where Lana and Shawn were born.

After Ron's discharge from the Marines, they moved to Cartwright where they lived in a mobile home, while farming with William and Grace. They rented the neighboring Izley farm, which they later purchased, along with several other neighboring farms, as they expanded their operation. They have been farming for 41 years as of 2011.

Mavis is proud of her "wonderful close family," and the fact that their farm has grown from 16 acres of beets when they started to over 1100 acres today, with many other improvements over the years. They enjoy riding motorcycles, boating on the river, and traveling to warm tropical places in the winter. She especially enjoys sewing, including the art of quilting.

Mavis's family L to R, Shawn Berry, Tracy Berry, Luke Berry, Mavis, Will Berry, Ron Berry and Lana Sundhiem

Lana Rene Berry Sundheim

Lana was born in July 9, 1968. After elementary school and graduating from Fairview High School in 1986, she attended Dickinson State College (1986-87), Montana State University (1988-90), and completed a course in cosmetology (1987-88). She married Kendall Wade Sundheim May 25, 1991. They have two "fabulous Siamese cats," Frank and Ed!

Lana has worked as a hair stylist in Bozeman for 22 years, and Kendall has been self-employed as the proprietor of A-1 Auto Glass in Bozeman, also for 22 years. Lana's favorite forms of recreation and relaxation are quilting, baking, and hiking.

Shawn Samuel Berry

Shawn was born July 12, 1969, in Orange County, CA. He went to East Fairview Elementary School, and graduated from Fairview High School in 1987. He went on to Montana State University where he completed a degree in Agricultural Business with a minor in Economics. After college, he took a job with a large agricultural machinery company, Unverferth, and has been territorial manager for North Dakota, South Dakota, Montana, and Wyoming for 20 years, and Western Canada for 10 years. He married Tracy Lynn Horning June 18, 1993. Tracy was in sales with KXMD TV from August 1993 and until August 1995, and has been delivering mail for USPS since 2008.

They are proud of their great family of four children, Brett Victor, born February 2, 1996; Cole William, born April 7, 1998; Amber Lynn, born December 10, 1999; and Danielle Grace, born February 8, 2004. They enjoy boating, snowmobiling, motorcycling, motor home camping, hunting, and any kind of recreation with their kids.

Luke Edward Berry

Luke was born June 19, 1976, went to East Fairview Elementary School, graduated from Fairview High School in 1993, and earned a degree in Agricultural Business from Montana State University in 1998. Since college, Luke has farmed with his father, and grandfather, for fourteen years. He lived with, and helped care for, his grandfather, until his death. He has a daughter, Abigail Lynn, born July 3, 2006.

He enjoys fishing, boating, motorcycling, and traveling, as leisurely pursuits.

Will Leonard Berry

Will was born May 24, 1977, attended Elementary School in East Fairview, graduated from Fairview High School in 1994, and completed a degree in Agricultural Business at Montana State University in 1999. After college, Will worked for the Unverferth machinery company for five years, headquartered in Visalia, California, and then returned to Cartwright to farm with Ron and Luke for the last six years.

He enjoys motorcycle riding, boating, and travel, having made trips to South America, Central America, Australia, and other parts of the world.

Mavis' grandchildren: Abby, Dani, Brett, Cole, Amber

CHAPTER 5

CONCLUSIONS

The roots of the Clark family can be traced to 17th Century America, and the Lasseys to the late 19th Century, both with origins in Europe. Their story is of immigrants who took great risks to improve their lives, which they did very successfully—as homesteaders, and later, as prosperous farmers. Both families were large—Constant and Emalie had nine children, while Louie and Princess had six. The narrative in these pages thus includes only a small segment of the larger Lassey and Clark family contribution to the population and prosperity of North Dakota, Montana, and elsewhere.

The first generation had minimal education, eight years or less. Only Emalie Lassey had no formal education. In the second generation, most finished the eighth grade, as William did, and several completed high school. Only Grace and her sister, Beulah, had college educations. In the third generation, everyone finished high school, several had some college, and there was one college graduate (Bill). In the fourth generation (of the William and Grace Lassey clan), there are nine college graduates (Cindy, Tim, Dione, Maureen, Susan, Julie, Shawn, Luke, and Will), and three with post-graduate degrees (Dione, Susan, and Julie). The fifth generation is still forming, but already includes three degrees (Jenny, Julie Ann, Dan) and one graduate degree (Jenny). None of the sixth generation is yet quite old enough for college.

In the first generation, all were farmers. In the second generation, there were also teachers, implement dealers, factory workers, salesmen, restaurant workers, and at varying times, other occupations. In the third generation, there were few farmers, and a great diversity of other forms of employment. In the fourth and fifth generations, there are a still a few farmers, but most are otherwise engaged—quite a dramatic shift over time.

Most family members have remained in North Dakota and Montana, although one has moved to Arizona (Bill), another to Ohio (Dione) and another to Minnesota (Susan). Extensive travel around the U.S. and abroad is clearly a favorite past-time of many family members, as it was for William and Grace.

Contributing to the community was very important to the first generation, and has been for successive generations. Constant and Emalie were involved in the formation and development of Cartwright, Sioux Township and McKenzie County, over many years. Louie and Princess were similarly involved in Rawson and Alexander, and later in Savage, Montana. William and Grace made huge contributions to Cartwright, Fairview, McKenzie County, North Dakota, and the country, over their lifetime. Commitment to the community has continued with their children and grandchildren.

Camping and picnicking seem to be appealing to many members of the younger generations, as was true for their elders. Family picnics were a prominent feature of social life for both Lassey and Clark families over many years. More recently, family reunions of the William and Grace Lassey clan have revolved around camp-outs and picnics.

Another common interest is gardening—a favorite activity of Constant and Emilie, Louie and Princess, and certainly William and Grace. Marilyn and Mavis are great gardeners, as was Lila. Most of their daughters, as well as Bill's daughters, have followed the tradition.

These are examples of continuity of interests and activities—maintained in spite of the great changes in educational levels and occupations. The daily use of computers, cell phones, and other technology is now commonplace for the third, fourth, and fifth generations, but was of course largely unknown to the first two generations.

Possibly the most pronounced continuity between generations is strong family ties. As noted throughout the previous pages, the younger generations place great value on family social opportunities and occasional reunions—as was so clearly evident during the recent gathering of the clan before, during, and after the recent death of the family patriarch, William.

APPENDIX

SUMMARY OF WILLIAM AND
GRACE LASSEY GENERATIONS

First Generation:	William and Grace Lassey
Second Generation:	(4)
	Lila, Bill, Marilyn, Mavis
Third Generation:	(15)
	Linda, Charlene, Karen, Cindy, Tim
	Dione, Maureen
	Rodney, Susan, Carol, Julie
	Lana, Shawn, Luke, Will
Fourth Generation:	(23)
	Jodie, Jenny
	Michelle, Ryan
	Julie Ann, Shawn, Nicholas, Melissa
	Christopher, Whitney, Sarah, Amanda
	Mollie
	Rebecca, Brady, Jennifer, Daniel, Ashley
	Brett, Cole, Amber, Dani
	Abigail
Fifth Generation:	(16)
	Benjamin, Gavin, Hope, Emma, Grace
	Dustin, Brett, Nick, Alexander
	Ayden, Christopher, Carlee, Cole
	Brayden, Gabe, Millie

TOTAL DESCENDENTS OF WILLIAM AND GRACE AS OF 2011: 58